G000270661

by Rennie McOwan

LangSyne

PUBLISHING

WRITING *to* REMEMBER

Lang**Syne**

PUBLISHING

WRITING *to* REMEMBER

79 Main Street, Newtongrange,
Midlothian EH22 4NA
Tel: 0131 344 0414   Fax: 0845 075 6085
E-mail: info@lang-syne.co.uk
www.langsyneshop.co.uk

Design by Dorothy Meikle
Printed by Printwell Ltd
© Lang Syne Publishers Ltd 2017

ISBN 978-1-85217-072-1

MacIntyre

SEPT NAMES INCLUDE:
MacCosham
MacTear
Mactier
Tyre
Wright

MacIntyre

MOTTO:
Per Ardua –
(Through Difficulties).

CREST:
A dexter hand holding
a dagger in pale Proper.

PLANT BADGE:
White Heather.

TERRITORY:
Glen Noe, on the shores of Loch Etive,
Argyll; Glen Orchy, close to the east end
of Loch Awe; parts of Breadalbane.

Chapter one:

The origins of the clan system

by Rennie McOwan

The original Scottish clans of the Highlands and the great families of the Lowlands and Borders were gatherings of families, relatives, allies and neighbours for mutual protection against rivals or invaders.

Scotland experienced invasion from the Vikings, the Romans and English armies from the south. The Norman invasion of what is now England also had an influence on land-holding in Scotland. Some of these invaders stayed on and in time became 'Scottish'.

The word clan derives from the Gaelic language term 'clann', meaning children, and it was first used many centuries ago as communities were formed around tribal lands in glens and mountain fastnesses.

The format of clans changed over the centuries, but at its best the chief and his family held the land on behalf of all, like trustees, and the ordinary clansmen and women believed they had a blood relationship with the founder of their clan.

There were two way duties and obligations. An inadequate chief could be deposed and replaced by someone of greater ability.

Clan people had an immense pride in race. Their relationship with the chief was like adult children to a father and they had a real dignity.

The concept of clanship is very old and a more feudal notion of authority gradually crept in.

Pictland, for instance, was divided into seven principalities ruled by feudal leaders who were the strongest and most charismatic leaders of their particular groups.

By the sixth century the 'British' kingdoms of Strathclyde, Lothian and Celtic Dalriada (Argyll) had emerged and Scotland, as one nation, began to take shape in the time of King Kenneth MacAlpin.

Some chiefs claimed descent from

ancient kings which may not have been accurate in every case.

By the twelfth and thirteenth centuries the clans and families were more strongly brought under the central control of Scottish monarchs.

Lands were awarded and administered more and more under royal favour, yet the power of the area clan chiefs was still very great.

The long wars to ensure Scotland's independence against the expansionist ideas of English monarchs extended the influence of some clans and reduced the lands of others.

Those who supported Scotland's greatest king, Robert the Bruce, were awarded the territories of the families who had opposed his claim to the Scottish throne.

In the Scottish Borders country – the notorious Debatable Lands – the great families built up a ferocious reputation for providing warlike men accustomed to raiding into England and occasionally fighting one another.

Chiefs had the power to dispense justice and to confiscate lands and clan warfare produced a society where martial virtues – courage, hardiness, tenacity – were greatly admired.

Gradually the relationship between the clans and the Crown became strained as Scottish monarchs became more orientated to life in the Lowlands and, on occasion, towards England.

The Highland clans spoke a different language, Gaelic, whereas the language of Lowland Scotland and the court was Scots and in more modern times, English.

Highlanders dressed differently, had different customs, and their wild mountain land sometimes seemed almost foreign to people living in the Lowlands.

It must be emphasised that Gaelic culture was very rich and story-telling, poetry, piping, the clarsach (harp) and other music all flourished and were greatly respected.

Highland culture was different from other parts of Scotland but it was not inferior or less sophisticated.

Central Government, whether in London or Edinburgh, sometimes saw the Gaelic clans as

Clan warfare produced a society where courage and tenacity were greatly admired

a challenge to their authority and some sent expeditions into the Highlands and west to crush the power of the Lords of the Isles.

Nevertheless, when the eighteenth century Jacobite Risings came along the cause of the Stuarts was mainly supported by Highland clans.

The word Jacobite comes from the Latin for James – Jacobus. The Jacobites wanted to restore the exiled Stuarts to the throne of Britain.

The monarchies of Scotland and England became one in 1603 when King James VI of Scotland (1st of England) gained the English throne after Queen Elizabeth died.

The Union of Parliaments of Scotland and England, the Treaty of Union, took place in 1707.

Some Highland clans, of course, and Lowland families opposed the Jacobites and supported the incoming Hanoverians.

After the Jacobite cause finally went down at Culloden in 1746 a kind of ethnic cleansing took place. The power of the chiefs was curtailed. Tartan and the pipes were banned in law.

Many emigrated, some because they

wanted to, some because they were evicted by force. In addition, many Highlanders left for the cities of the south to seek work.

Many of the clan lands became home to sheep and deer shooting estates.

But the warlike traditions of the clans and the great Lowland and Border families lived on, with their descendants fighting bravely for freedom in two world wars.

Remember the men from whence you came, says the Gaelic proverb, and to that could be added the role of many heroic women.

The spirit of the clan, of having roots, whether Highland or Lowland, means much to thousands of people.

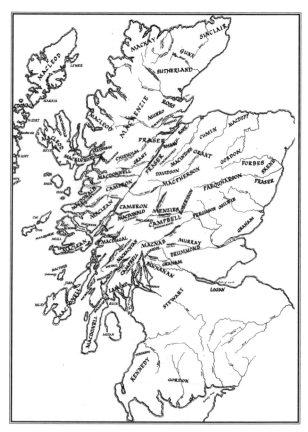

A map of the clans' homelands

Chapter two:

Settling scores

The clans have gone now from that rich corner at the east end of Loch Awe, in Argyll, where the MacGregors were once the custodians of the great keep of Kilchurn Castle and where their townships dotted Glen Streae and Glen Orchy, but traces remain among the grass and heather of the hillsides.

The Glen Orchy Campbells, who evolved into the powerful house of Breadalbane, pushed the MacGregors eastwards and also began to impose over-lordship on the clans and families in the area and one of these was the MacIntyres, the clan which produced one of the best nature poets, Duncan Ban MacIntyre (1724-1812), Donnachadh Ban nan Oran, Fair-Duncan-of-the-Songs.

There is a striking, Grecian-style monument to him on a knoll close to the village of Dalmally. It was erected in 1859 and money for it came from Gaelic exiles all over the world.

The Forestry Commission has made a road from close to the village to the foot of the monument and it is a splendid viewpoint over Loch Awe and also over the lower ground and across to the great mountain, Ben Cruachan, Cruachan Beann, the-heaped-up-mountain-of-the-many-tops.

Just to the east of Ben Cruachan's strung out mass lie two other prominent peaks, Beinn Eunaich (Fowling Mountain) and Beinn a' Chochuill (of the hood or shell). Between them and Ben Cruachan lies a sloping glen and a prominent burn.

The landscape in much of the area has changed from past centuries with much, ugly, conifer forestry, with lines of pylons and a metalled track running up the east side of this glen and which is linked to modern hydro electric schemes.

The crest of the bealach or pass lies just beyond the end of this hydro road and a little line of poles runs up and over the crest.

In this corner of the upper glen, below the crest of the pass and close to the end of this hydro 'road', lies a large boulder which has been partly split in two by the action of frost and ice and many winter storms. It is flattish in shape and has the look of a table.

In fact, it was used as such once a year by the MacIntyres in special ceremonies whose roots go back into the centuries and which emphasises the special significance given to the colour white long ago.

It meant guardianship, protection and security and it may be why the MacIntyres plant badge is white heather (although some sources only say heather).

Plant badges of the clans were not, of course, for identification as is often said, but were talismans and meant something special. In the MacIntyres case white was indeed very special, as we shall see shortly.

In Gaelic the name MacIntyre is rendered Mac an t-Saoir, meaning Son of the Carpenter. There is a strong tradition which says that Olaf the Red, King of (the island of) Man and Somerled, Thane of Argyll, were sailing in their galleys near to one another on a raiding foray.

Somerled had earlier asked for the hand of Olaf's daughter in marriage, but Oaf refused. Somerled's nephew, Maurice MacNaill sailed in Olaf's galley and he decided to give his uncle a helping hand. Maurice secretly bored a number of holes in Olaf's galley that night as the two craft lay side by side at anchor and overlaid the holes with tallow and butter.

The next day the galleys sailed south from the island of Skye, where they had been moored and when off the long peninsula of Ardnamurchan, Olaf's galley began to sink.

Olaf called to Somerled for help, but Somerled said he would only assist him on condition that he was given the hand in marriage of Olaf's daughter.

Olaf at first refused, but as the water began to lap about his ankles and finding himself in great peril he gave his consent. Somerled then gleefully helped him to leave his sinking ship and to clamber to safety aboard Somerled's galley.

When Olaf could no longer see what was happening on his own galley, Maurice MacNiall quickly plugged the holes with wooden pins he had in readiness. Olaf's galley was saved and from that day Maurice MacNiall was known as An t-Saoir, the Carpenter, and his descendants as Mac an t-Saoir, Son of the Carpenter.

The great Highland historian, writer and naturalist, the late Seton Gordon, wrote that the

Somerled in action against the enemy

MacIntyres came to Loch Etive around the 14th century.

There was a Gaelic saying, "The two oldest farmers in Alba (Scotland) are the apple tree which grows on the shore of Loch Etive and MacIntyre of Glen Noe".

Glen Noe (Nodha), means the new glen, and partly connects Loch Etive and the east end of Loch Awe by means of the main pass where the flat stone stands and which is called the Lairig Nodha, the New Pass.

An old legend has it that the original home of the MacIntyres might have been in the Hebrides. One tradition favours Skye, anoher the island of Islay (pronounced eye-la) and another (less strong) the peninsula of Kintyre.

The clan went walkabout, as the Australians say, and when they approached Ben Cruachan from the south-west and driving their cattle with them – a tale which gives evidence to Islay as the place of origin – they met a Spectre called the Spirit of Cruachan.

This mountain long ago was thought to be

the home of witches and spectral beings and its twin peaks were 'looked to' by kings and leaders from the rock-fortress of Dunadd, near the modern Crinan Canal and south of Oban, the cradle of Scotland.

The Spirit of Cruachan barred their way to test their courage and when she was satisfied with the MacIntyres bravery she became friendly and guided them to the most suitable passes. The Spirit told them that they were to make their new home where a white cow in their herd, and which they treasured as a sacred beast, would lie down after the crossing of the Lairig Nodha.

They did so, possibly in the autumn, and they struck strong winds and harsh terrain.

It must have been a great joy for them the see the green shores of Loch Etive below them and fringing oak, birch and alder woods in the lower glen. They descended towards the loch shore and about half a mile away from the water the white cow lay down.

The MacIntyres set up home there and prospered for five centuries.

About this time King Robert the Bruce was fighting for the throne of Scotland and had defeated the MacDougalls in the Pass of Brander which runs alongside loch Awe.

The MacDougalls lost their lands and area-control to the Stewarts who had aided Bruce. The MacIntyres became 'foresters' to the Stewarts and at a later date to the Campbells.

(The word 'forester' is more like our modern game wardens: they controlled the hunting of red deer. The words deer forest have nothing to do with trees, but are a corruption of Latin for the land-outwith-the-enclosure.)

The MacIntyres held Glen Noe on a tenant basis from the Campbells of Inverawe and the flat stone near the crest of the Lairig Nodha was of great symbolic importance.

At midsummer a snowball was brought from a corrie (hollow) on Ben Cruachan, known as the Snowy Corry, Cor' an t-Sneachda, and brought to the stone.

A white calf was handed over with

ceremony to the Campbells and a kind of barbecue was held at this stone, called the Stone-of-the-Fatted-Calf, Clach an Laoigh Bhaita. The MacIntyres paid their rent in the normal way by supplying men-at-arms or meal or money, but the snowball was a sign of their security of tenure.

In the graveyard of Ardchattan priory, on the shores of Loch Etive, are the graves of some of the MacIntyre chiefs and one has a round carving on it like a ball or orb and this may commemorate the snowball ceremony.

But this old custom was all to go sour. The Campbells gradually increased the money rent until, in time, the MacIntyres could no longer pay it and they left Glen Noe in the early 1890s.

Not a lot is known about the MacIntyre chiefs. It is known that one of them, Duncan, married Mary, daughter of Patrick Campbell of Barcaldine. James, the bard chief, born in 1727, and described in old documents as Seumas Mac an t-Saoir, Fear a Ghleinne Nodha, became an excellent Gaelic scholar and was helped in his education by the Earl of Breadalbane. He wrote many verses sending up Dr. Samuel Johnson because that ponderous literary figure said the Highlanders were a rude barbarous people.

The chief was visited by Duncan Ban MacIntyre who wrote a poem about his visit to Glen Noe and who described the MacIntyres great seal which had eagles displaying wings and a ship with sails. The chief died in 1799 and his wife lived to an age of 103.

When the old days in Glen Noe and Loch Etive-side came to an end and the last MacIntyres emigrated to the United States they preserved the clan's armorial great seal, signet ring and quaffing cup.

In 1955 Alasdair MacIntyre of Camus-na-h-Einidh recorded arms in the Lyon Court, Scotland's court for heraldic matters, as cadet of the chiefly house of MacIntyre.

The shield was different from that which some clan historians believed to be correct and in 1991 James Wallace MacIntyre of Glen Noe, ninth of the recorded chiefs, matriculated the correct 'undifferenced arms'.

Chapter three:

Tales and legend

The MacIntyres got around. A branch is sometimes recorded as a sept of the Campbells of Craignish. MacIntyre in Badenoch are descended from the bard whom William, 13th of Mackintosh, took under his protection in 1496.

A family of MacIntyres were hereditary pipers to MacDonald of Clan Ranald and the MacIntyres of Rannoch were hereditary pipers to the chief of Clan Menzies.

A branch of the clan resident in Cladich, near Loch Awe, were renowned for their weaving of hose (stockings) and garters.

A sept of Glen Noe settled at Camus na-h-Eiridh, probably during the 15th century, and is regarded by many as the most ancient of the cadet branches.

Although the MacIntyres were under Campbell over-lordship many of them joined the army of James Graham, Marquis of Montrose, and his redoubtable second in command, that great soldier Alasdair MacColla, the warleader of Clan Donald, in their bid to win Scotland for Charles I.

The 17th century wars of the Covenant are complex events with links to England and Ireland and involving both religious and political issues.

Alasdair MacColla was also striving to ensure Clan Donald held onto the Headship of the Gael in the face of the expansionist Campbells. He also fought for the Roman Catholic cause against the mainly Presbyterian alliance, the Solemn League and Covenant, and he was the greatest of the sword-and-buckler men and the Achilles of the Gael.

The royal army burned all houses in Campbell terrain, but the MacIntyres were left untouched because of ancient links with Clan Donald.

There is an evocative picture of a deer belling (roaring) in Glen Noe in author Neil

Munro's historical novel, "John Splended", which tells of these wars.

He describes the mainly Campbell army sleeping in Glen Noe on their way north to try and trap Montrose and Alasdair MacColla, but who were to be routed in the terrible defeat at Inverlochy, near modern Fort William, in 1645.

One or two MacIntyres were present on the Campbell side possibly to guard against changes in fortunes.

The chief's piper joined Montrose's army with some clansmen, but the chief himself was with the Duke of Argyll at Inverlochy. He must have regretted it.

Seton Gordon states that the MacIntyres once possessed ancient manuscripts about the House of Uisneach (pronounced wish-na) who were linked to one of the oldest sagas in Scotland and Ireland and who heroes and heroine had lived beside Loch Etive.

The old tale comes in several versions and was once known from Barra to Cowal and a

lovely song exists called 'Deirdre's Farewell to
Scotland' in which the verses tell of her longing in
exile for the glens, Glen Massan, Glen Da Rua
(modern Glendaruel) and Glen Etive.

Deirdre was the Celtic Helen and was
reputed to be one of the loveliest women in the
world. Her name means Drop of Dew and should
be pronounced jeer-dre, but hardly ever is.

A mainstream version of the old story
was that Deirdre was brought up at the court of
king Conochbar or Cormac in Ireland. The king
desired her, but she did not reciprocate his
feelings. She was reputed to be a Child of
Destiny and would play a part in bringing down
the House of King of Ulster.

Deirdre fell in love with a warrior called
Naoise (pronounced noy-sha), of the House of
Uisneach, and the lovers fled to Scotland along
with Naoise's brothers, Aluinn and Ardan, and
they lived a life of Golden Age joy in the
Scottish glens.

They had a bower in Glen Etive, probably
near Dalness, and its walls were covered in the

down of birds and its floors in deer hides and it was possible to catch salmon from its windows because it was sited close to deep pools in the Highland river.

The story is commemorated in several place names in Scotland. Loch Ness may take its name from Naoise.

King Cormac sent a mutual friend, Fergus, to Scotland and he persuaded the lovers to return to Ireland where they were promised safety.

There is a stone in Aird's Bay, near Taynuilt, called the Stone of Farewell, which is reputed to mark the spot where the royal barge carried Fergus, Naoise and Deirdre back to Ireland.

Naoise was then killed by the vengeful King Cormac. Deirdre either committed suicide or was also killed. Her death meant that tribal fighting broke out and eventually brought about the fall of the House of Ulster, thus fulfilling the prophecy.

If the MacIntyres did indeed possess these ancient manuscripts, as Seton Gordon claims, then their loss is grievous indeed.

Chapter four:

A guiding light

When Prince Charles Edward Stuart raised the Jacobite standard at Glenfinnan 1745, the last fling of the exiled Stuarts to win back the throne of Britain from the incoming House of Hanover, there were MacIntyres in the Jacobite ranks. They fought alongside the Stewarts of Appin who had many casualties in the terrible defeat at Culloden in 1746.

James, the third chief, wanted to be there, but his Campbell wife and neighbours persuaded him not to.

Duncan Ban MacIntyre fought on the Hanovarian side at the battle of Falkirk in 1756 which the Jacobites unexpectadly won, but he was there under duress and in place of another man.

He threw away his sword and wrote a sarcastic song/poem about it and his real sympathies lay with the Jacobites. He lamented the great changes in Highland life, the banning of the tartan and of the pipes by the victorious Hanovarians.

In modern times there has been a new interest in Duncan Ban MacIntyre. The Gaelic Society of Inverness erected a cairn to him at his birthplace at Druim Luighart, near Inveroran, in the Blackmount, and not far from the site of the old inn where he met his wife, Mairi Ban Og, Fair Young Mary. He wrote of her that her breath was as sweet as apples.

He also lived for a time near Dalness and he had another house in Auch Glen, and Ais an t-Sithein, Back-of-the-Faery-Hill, and close to his favourite mountain, Ben Dorain (Beinn Dobhrain), about which he wrote his most famous song/poem, 'In Praise of Ben Dorain'.

It is written in the movements of pibroch, rather like a classical music symphony, with different movements when the speed and tempo change. Pibroch is the classical music of the bagpipes, and extremely sensitive and precise musical art form. Only the best pipers can play pibroch and only a handful can play a pibroch theme faultlessly.

It was natural for Duncan Ban to use that form for his poem because it was a normal part of his Gaelic heritage of poems, songs, stories, the clarsach (the Highland harp) and the bagpipes.

Duncan Ban was illiterate in the sense that he could not read and he could barely write his own name.

But he was entirely literate in the old Gaelic oral traditions of the Highlands where people could remember and recite thousands of words of poetry of songs without a slip or a stutter.

Like all of his generation, he was immersed in Gaelic culture, the rich folklore heritage which ranged from plants and trees having a spirit life to knolls, burns and woods which were full of sites connected with the great Fingalian heroes and heroines of the past and tales of witches, warlocks, kelpies and faeries.

But he was also a practical man and his poem about Ben Dorian tells about the landscape of the time and about firearms. He hated the coming of the sheep and the removal of people from ancient lands in the name of profit.

Duncan wrote an evocative poem called "The Misty Corrie" which is sited in long Glen Lochay, to the west of Killin, in Perthshire, and where red deer calves are born to this day.

Duncan Ban later moved to Edinburgh with his wife where he joined the City Guard. He was a familiar figure to the Gaels who had flocked to Scotland's capital in search of work.

He dictated his poems to friends and after they were published he became famous and he and Mairi toured the Highlands. School pupils were given the day off to see him and to hear his poems being read.

Like several Highland clans, the MacIntyres possessed a charm stone which doubled as a talisman and a cure for illnesses.

The people long ago had an affinity with stone and were known to stand and touch the surface of prominent boulders as if they could sense vibrations within.

Healing stones for different diseases were

not uncommon, such as the famous stones of St Fillan which can be seen in the folklore visitor centre in Killin or specially shaped standing stones or boulders. Some caves, too, were special in character and were regarded as entrances to the other world.

Dr Robert McIntyre, a retired chest consultant and former Provost of Stirling, was the first Scottish National Party Member of Parliament to be elected to the House of Commons. He was president of the S.N.P., a man who has done much for Scotland, and is proud of his MacIntyre heritage.

And there are MacIntyres abroad whose forebears knew the White Calf and the New Glen and this small clan lives on in spirit. It contributed much to Highland life and totally deserves its honoured place.